CONVERSATIONS FOR THE JOURNEY

40 ways for you to build sporting character

By Richard Shorter

NON-PERFECT
DAD
.CO.UK

Conversations for the Journey
40 ways for you to build sporting character
Copyright © 2018 Richard Shorter

Published by Shorter Thumb Books
Greenhill Manse
Aylsham Lane
Harold Hill
Essex RM3 7YL

British Library cataloguing in Publication Data

ISBN 978-1-9164647-0-4

Cover design, typeset and print management by
DJE Creative, Westcliff-on-Sea, Essex | www.djecreative.co.uk

Contents

Questions

The big four

Deepening the parent/child relationship

Enhancing sideline support

Big picture questions

Giving a positive understanding of self

Nurturing a great team member

Building self-awareness

Questions to pose on the way home

Bonus question

Endorsements

'All of us want the best for our own children and others we teach or coach. How we do this is not always obvious or easy - this easy to read guide opens up the potential for us to be better at supporting those children... I am off to ask the Top Trumps question to my 14-year-old son!'
John Mallett, Director of Rugby, Millfield School

'Richard's focus on developing the character of your child, whether that be on or off the pitch, will be fundamental to fostering a relationship of honesty, warmth, and nurturance between yourself and them.'
Dr Suzanne Brown (DClinPsy, MSci, BSci), Clinical Psychologist, Director of Emotionally Connected - www.emotionallyconnected.co.uk

'For me, the key learning from reading this book has been to take a moment, reflect on the impact what I say next will have long term on my son, and to enjoy the role of being a dad and relish the challenge of the conversations.'
Andy Hurry, Director of Cricket, Somerset County Cricket Club

'Richard draws on his extensive experience to offer a useful primer that I know many parents and their children will value. My favourite question is No.39.'
Dr Edward T. Hall, Senior Lecturer in Sports Coaching

'He delivered in the England Rugby performance pathway on a number of occasions on topics such as supporting the journey from dependence to independence, relationships with coaches, parents' roles in a performance programme and good questions to ask around sport and in particular the games. The feedback from the parents was always very strong.'
Fletch, The Magic Academy – Formally England Rugby U18 head coach

'A must-read for any parents whose children enjoy sport, not just those pursuing professionalism.'
TW Taylor, Head of Rugby, New Hall School

'As a dad myself, this is extremely useful.'
Kevin Mannion, Academy Performance Manager, Gloucester Rugby

'A great tool that will lead to a deeper awareness of one another. Listening and understanding each other are key skills, in not only sport but in all walks of life.'
Amelea Lancaster, Player Management & Academy Team, Saracens Rugby

'The all-conquering New Zealand Rugby Union Team state, "Better People make Better All-Blacks", and this book will help all of us parents to maximise the impact of each sporting car journey as we support the growth of our very own "Better Person".'
Mark Garaway, Director of Cricket, Millfield

'An essential guide for any parent of sporting children… some of the best ideas I have seen written on this subject. A must-read!!'
Gary Street, Harlequins Rugby
Academy Coach Development Officer & Women's Head Coach

'If you think you don't need any of these... you've probably only been listening to one side of the conversation!'
Anastacia Long, Trinity School, Croydon

'Richard cuts through the fog to create a reflective learning and sharing toolkit that will empower parents to connect their athletes with the "bigger picture".'
Craig 'Gunny' Gunn (www.craiggunn.org)

'A definite must-read for any sporting parent and in particular any parent coach. For me, it has been 18 years of trial and error without any framework - you have provided that in abundance.'
Parent of England U18 Rugby player

Introduction

Thank you.

Thank you for all the car journeys to and from training, and for all the games. Thank you for the meals packed and the smelly sports gear washed. The lie-ins you have given up and the money you have spent to enable your child to do sport.

We know that parents love supporting their children in playing sport and that this has many highs and lows. I've been told many times – and this is also supported by research – that the car journey to and from sporting activities causes parents significant challenges. These include the long journeys after a loss, the trips after a family row about homework and traveling to matches that are subsequently cancelled on arrival because of bad weather. Then there's the challenge of trying to talk to a 'moody' teen and always getting the question wrong, and the pain of sitting next to a child who has sat on the bench for an entire game. Car journeys can be great and they can suck. I know, as I've done enough of them with my kids.

But car journeys also offer an opportunity. In today's time-poor world, they give us parents quality time with our offspring. They are stuck in the car and so we have a captive audience! My gift to you is 40 conversation starters that will make these car journeys an effective parenting tool, enabling you to nurture and shape your child's character for success both on and off the sports field.

Picture your child many years from now. What's important to you about who they become in later life? What sort of partner do you want them to be? How do you imagine they will parent your grandchildren? How will they look after you in old age? My guess is you are thinking about their character and not a full trophy cabinet. There is nothing wrong with winning or being competitive – visit my house to see a competitive dad and his kids play! – but it's your child's character that will enable them to be their best and enjoy the most important roles they will have in life. And yes, character is also key to lasting sporting success. It enables a player to continuously engage in the competitive process of self-improvement and perform well under pressure. As Sir Alex Ferguson, someone who knew a little about winning, said in his book *Leading*: "If I had to choose between someone who had great talent but was short on grit and desire and another player who was good but had great determination and drive, I would always prefer the latter."

Have you ever considered that as a parent you have more influence on your child's character than any other person in their life? As a dad of three, I feel the weight of that responsibility. And, as someone who has supported parents for 20 years, I know that being a mum or dad isn't easy. I also know that all parent-child relationships are unique and that the last thing any parent wants is someone interfering with this most important role.

So this book does not give you 40 answers but rather 40 questions. It is a companion designed to nudge you into having the beneficial conversations on the journey to or from sports fixtures, down the phone or over Skype, that will enable you and your child to develop your relationship and stay focused on what is important – character. The character needed for highs and lows in the sporting journey today and for success in all parts of life tomorrow.

Enjoy!

What this conversation companion will do

- Provide a framework for you to have significant conversations with your child that will make a difference.
- Nudge you into thinking about what will help develop your child's mindset and character, and give you the space to think about how you can best support them.
- Give you many tools to explore both your and your child's wonderful uniqueness.
- Provide your child with a voice in conversations, which you and they may not have found before.
- Help you laugh, cry and enjoy all the other wonderful parts of being human together.
- Place high value on the character and mindset that helps with success in sport and in life.
- Help you give the message to your child that you love them and want to listen to them and support them as they grow and thrive as an individual.

All the questions are offered here to help you maximise your impact on your children and their characters. They are based on my experience of supporting parents, being a parent myself, and the latest academic research – please visit non-perfectdad.co.uk/40 for more details and resources.

How to use this conversation companion

Some tips to help you get the most from this conversation companion:
- Don't try to ask all the questions at once!
- When the vibe is right, pick one question you feel comfortable with. Understand that sometimes your child will not want to talk – that's OK, simply try again another time. Sometimes they will respond defensively, and that's OK, too. Wait for them to calm down and try again. Questions 1 or 3 might be good ones to start with.
- Listen well to your child's answers – at times you will be blown away by their depth and insight – and reflect back what you think you've heard. Then ask another open question (a question without a simple yes or no answer).
- Before you ask a question, be honest with yourself and consider if you expect a specific answer – how will you feel if the answer is not one you want to hear?
- Most of the questions are written for children aged 11 to 18, but you might need to adapt the language to be more age-appropriate.
- To start with, you might feel a bit uncomfortable trying these conversations, but keep going. Like any skill, it requires practice. And remember, learning to have these key conversations is a process for your child as well as for you.
- Your child might think that some of the questions are a bit cringy or cheesy. That's OK. Play to it and have some fun together.
- If you were to only use a few conversations from the companion, use questions 1 to 4. Don't use them all at once, but employ them when needed and repeat regularly.
- Remember, character takes time to grow – these conversations may produce some quick wins, but the true fruit will develop over months and years.

The big four

1. This isn't about me

What do you want from me on game/training day?

Ways to ask

Your sport is really important to you, so I've been wondering what you want from me on game day/training day?

I want this (sport) to be yours, not mine, so...

As your mum/dad, I want to be as supportive as possible.

What to try and avoid

There are a few responses to this question that may reduce your child's ability to develop the character and mindset they'll need to be successful. You don't want to say yes to packing their bag, paying them for scoring or buying 'crap' sugar-filled food as a treat after the game. All of these will reduce the chances of getting what you want: a strong, resilient child.

What it will give

This question is all about hearing what our children want. As they grow and develop, their needs will change. This way you are checking in on what they want from their time in sport. Their fun and enjoyment, as well as their long-term engagement, are directly linked to how you engage with them.

2. Proud parents alert

Why do you think I am proud of you?

Ways to ask it

I've been thinking about how proud I am of you. Do you know why I'm proud of you? Life can be so busy and complicated, I'm wondering if in all the busyness you know why I'm proud of you?

What to try and avoid

Why are you proud of them? Do your children believe your pride in them is based on what they do or who they are? Focusing on their character will enable them to build on what fuels their growth. If they reply, "Because I'm big and strong," you can reply, "I'm proud of the way you are determined to use your strength." If they say, "Because I've scored loads of goals," you might offer, "I'm proud of how creative you are, which sometimes leads to goals."

What it will give

Children who think their parents' pride is based on results are more likely to believe they have to be good at stuff in order to make people happy. They are also more likely to think that their self-worth is not in who they are but in what they do. Now, life is confusing and it is hard to always get this right as parents. Reflect on their answers and where they might have heard these messages, either through you or at school.

3. But why?
Why do you play?

Ways to ask it
I really enjoyed seeing you play, it makes me feel so happy to watch you … it's great to see you play with a smile on your face. What's going through your mind then? Why do you play the game the way you do? You clearly love your sport. What are the main reasons why you play/take part? How important are friends to you? How much do you value fun/teamwork? If you could win, but not have fun, would you still play?

What to try and avoid
This is about hearing your child's voice and understanding their motivation. The reality is that if fun and enjoyment are not high on the list, your child is going to struggle with the highs and lows of sport. If they don't mention fun, you might want to explore why that is. If they do and you think winning or being a champion should be a higher priority, perhaps you can explore with them why those successes are not as critical to them and reflect on your own reasons for placing such importance on them. Try to avoid projecting your reasons for why they play onto them.

What it will give
I want my children to love their sport and to remain involved with it for decades to come. This question is all about motivating and helping our children remain loving towards their sport. Listening carefully to their answers will help fuel your support and increase their love of the game. As parents, it is normal for us to become invested in the outcome of our children's sporting activities, but for most kids this is less important. Understanding what part of the sport is fun for them will help you shape your support and behaviour around their voice.

4. Contrite parents
I'm sorry

Ways to ask it

Parenting is hard. I'm called the *Non*-Perfect Dad for a reason. I often get it wrong! Sometimes we handle the pressure of sport and parenting poorly, and need to start the conversation with something like, "I've been thinking about the way I was when …"/"I'm not sure I'm getting the balance right, I'm sorry."/"Here is what I'm going to try in the future."/"Sorry for x, how do you think I can get better at x?"

What to try and avoid

This is not a guilt trip, nor is it to keep the word sorry on repeat like some kind of social media GIF that never stops. This is about restoring your relationship and moving forward.

What it will give

The sports journey is not a straightforward path for either a child or their parent. Possessing the humility to reflect, restore and move forward is a gift to your relationship, and to helping your child understand the human condition. Some people say sorry too often and some don't say it enough. Building character means accepting our part in the conflict, offering restoration and then moving forward.

Deepening the parent/child relationship

5. How will Mum and Dad be scored?

What do you think will make you proud of me today?

Ways to ask it

I love watching you play, as it makes me so proud, but what will make you proud of me today? It is important to me that I'm giving you the right support, so what will make you pleased with me?

What to try and avoid

Don't get defensive if the answers are a bit painful. Think about them and ask for more detail later. Don't be surprised if the answers are short, such as, "Don't embarrass me!" Try and follow up short responses, but don't push it. If they mention what they'd rather you wouldn't do (such as shouting instructions from the sideline) and you want to carry on doing it, try to put yourself in their shoes. Remind yourself whose sport this is.

What it will give

This will give you a great lowdown on your child's hopes for your behaviour before, during and after the game. You'll then have a better framework to provide them with the game day they are hoping for.

6. Off-the-chart enjoyment

What makes your game day fun?

Ways to ask it

I'm interested to know what makes your game day fun? What would need to happen for it to score a 10 out of 10? How would your teammates act? How would your coach treat you? How could I behave to enable your day to be the best?

What to try and avoid

You know your child better than anyone, but as parents we can make many assumptions about what 'fun' is for our children. One child played golf because they enjoyed the feeling of the swing and went on to become a British champion! Try not to impose your understanding and idea of fun onto your child. Listen and ask open questions, which will give you more information.

What it will give

To keep going at anything in life, we need to know why we are doing it and what motivates us. Fun is such a broad concept. This question will remind your child about why they play. It will also provide you with the words to say on those hard days, such as when they are 'cut' from a team or injured, because you can then gently point out what they do get from the game.

7. My biggest crash and burn

What do you think I learned from my biggest failure or mistake?

Ways to ask it

Learning from painful experiences is the only way to grow. Do you
know what your (Mum's/Dad's) biggest failure was? (Tell them.)
What do you think I learnt from it? What would have helped me to
find the courage to learn from it? If you were my best friend and I'd
just told you what had happened to me, what would you have said?

What to try and avoid

Our example matters, whether we did or didn't learn from our
'biggest' fail. So don't discount your story as invalid, as it can still be
of help to your child. Think carefully about which story you tell them.
You may not be ready to talk about some things, so only share what
you are ready to open up about.

What it will give

This is a great opportunity to help your children learn from your
character. If you handled the mess well, they will hear that. But they
will still learn loads if you are humble enough to share with them that
you didn't cope with it well. This will give them an insight into how
being willing to learn from challenges is a massive asset.

8. I'm your parent, not your slave!

When would it be most helpful for you to take responsibility for your own sporting arrangements?

Ways to ask it

Helping you enjoy your sport means helping you take responsibility over your participation. When will it be right for you to pack your bag, contact the coach, wash your kit and go hunting for lost property? You are growing up and with that comes responsibility. Having the right mindset is all about taking leadership of yourself.

What to try and avoid

Every child over 10 can begin to take responsibility for their own sporting participation. We do our child's potential sporting success and character development no favours by doing everything for them. Instead, we are helping them to avoid the pain that comes with not taking responsibility. Do yourself and your child a favour and let them learn this now. We've all worked with someone who needs to be spoon-fed as an adult. At the same time, please don't just announce that they now have to do everything for themselves – help them learn how to do it.

What it will give

This will give your child a chance to take more ownership of their sports journey, and experience what it is to forget! Most coaches would prefer that you let them stumble this way because it builds the right character. (That said, some children seem to take more stumbles to learn than others, and that's OK too.)

9. Parents who coach

How was the coach (AKA me) today?

Before we get into this further, I want to say thank you. Without parents coaching their children, grassroots sport doesn't happen. When you arrive at the training pitch, tell your child you are taking off your parent's hat and putting on your coach's hat.

Ways to ask it
I'm changing hats now – off goes the coach's hat and back on goes the parent's one. So, how was the coach today? What did they do well? How could they have been better?

What to try and avoid
This could be painful, and you are opening yourself up to criticism. Take some deep breaths and keep listening. Then talk to someone trusted later on.

What it will give
This will give your relationship as a parent priority over your relationship as a coach and athlete, which, let's face it, is the more important one. You can make it playful and fun. I can't promise this will always be easy, but it will lay the foundation for showing what humility of character looks like and how different roles have different impacts on who we are and our relationships.

Enhancing sideline support

10. Mannerism madness

Can you show me what my body language is like when ...?

Ways to ask it

(This is going to sound strange, but humour me.) When you are playing, can you show me what I look like when you think I'm happy with you? Just by looking at me, can you tell how I'm feeling on the touchline when you're playing? Can you show me what I'm like when you think I'm cross or frustrated with you? How does this make you feel?

What to try and avoid

It can be tough to hear what others think about what we look like, but our body language has a massive impact on those we love. Avoid making it too serious and reenact what they say in exaggerated ways in order to keep it fun. It is also worth remembering that sometimes it's hard to tell how a person is feeling from their body language. If your child perceives something negative about you which you don't feel is a fair assessment, then this is a good opportunity to explore why that might be the case.

What it will give

We know we communicate much without words. The parent on the sideline can be 'screaming' emotions at their child without realising. This question will show you the impact of your unspoken communication and what you can work on to become more neutral. Our child's character can take a massive knock when we communicate frustration, disappointment or anger without saying a word.

11. Touchline madness!

What do you think I should do if I'm feeling stressed on the touchline?

Ways to ask it

I love watching you play, but the touchline can be a stressful place. What do you think I should do if I am feeling uncomfortable on the touchline? Sport creates wonderful emotional moments, but sometimes parents struggle with them. What do you think I should do if that happens?

What to try and avoid

As much as you wish Harry McGobbie's dad would SHUT UP on the sideline, this is not an opportunity to talk at length about Harry's dad or how bad the refs are. Confrontation on the side of the sports pitch during a game is really unhelpful. If your child suggests a sideline dispute, talk about why that will be unhelpful and explore better ways to resolve it … such as in the bar over a pint (the parents, not the kids!).

What it will give

I have yet to meet an honest sports parent who hasn't felt uncomfortable at some point on the side of the pitch. This is a great way to talk about the challenges and what you can do about them. Your child will add valuable insights that will help you decide how to act.

12. Noise pollution
What impact do sideline comments have on you while you play?

Ways to ask it
I am curious about the impact sideline comments have on your game and mindset? How do they make you feel when you play? Can you hear the positive comments? Can you hear the negative ones? If so, what effect do they have? Can you hear me on the touchline?
Be honest, do my comments help?

What to try and avoid
This is not an easy question to ask if you are really vocal. You'll need to make it clear that you really want to hear what they have to say. For a variety of reasons, I advise that instructions from the sideline are really unhelpful, so it might be worth exploring things further if they say they do find it beneficial. What does it say about the character of a child if they need instructions every time they get the ball?

What it will give
Our presence has a massive impact on the way our children experience their game day and training. Learning to adjust our own behaviour means that we can enable them to have more fun and enjoy their sport for the right reasons. Kids love it when we watch them, but reserving our noise for encouraging everyone can only lead to a better game-day experience for all involved, even if that means we need to bite our tongue sometimes!

13. Sports MasterChef

What can I teach you to cook for game day?

Ways to ask it

What would your favourite food be to prep for a game? How will that food be helpful for your body and your performance? Would you like to learn how to cook good game day food? If you were on the MasterChef TV programme and your brief was to cook an excellent and nutritious game day meal, what would you make?

What to try and avoid

Every parent knows the 'Battle of the Greens'. You don't need me to tell you that getting kids to make wise choices about food can be a major battleground. This question is not about creating a food fight, it's about asking our children to reflect on their eating habits and what Mum and Dad can do to support their nutritional needs. If you're not sure what is healthy for growing athletes, have a look on the web or ask your club for guidance. They should be providing this advice for young athletes.

What it will give

Talking about food can be a challenge, and I know some kids develop habits that we'd prefer them to change. However, they are still children and having this conversation is a way to open up this particular discussion in a positive way around your shared passion of sport. Your children are going to need to cook for themselves when they leave home, so this gives you an excuse to try and get them in the kitchen with you.

Big picture questions

14. Family likeness

Who in the family are you most like?

Ways to ask it

As a family, we've given so much to each other. Who do you think you are most like – your mum or your dad?

Who have you inherited your sense of humour from? What about your creativity or your organisational skills? Think about the way you approach a challenge, conflict or failure. How would you change or improve on the faults/qualities you see in us?

What to try and avoid

This is not a 'who is the better parent?' contest. This is about inspiring reflection concerning what we are like, where we learn our character traits from and what we would change if we could. Avoid being hurt if they spot something you'd rather not confront. This isn't about you, it's about your child's awareness of who they are, their strengths and what is needed to move forward.

What it will give

The apple doesn't fall far from the tree, but it can be moved! This question will provide keen self-awareness. Success comes from knowing ourselves.

15. The Generation Game

Can you guess what Grandma and Grandpa were like before big games (or pressure moments) with me?

Ways to ask it

As I try my best to support you, can you guess what your grandparents were like at supporting me? From what you know about their character, what do you think they were like? How do you think I responded to their support? How do you think their support affected me? What differences do you think there are between the way my parents supported me and how they now support you? Why do you think there is that difference? (If possible, have the grandparents in the room when you ask these questions.)

What to try and avoid

This isn't about shaming grandparents or suggesting that our children have it easier or harder. This is about encouraging reflection, which leads to learning and gratitude. Avoid feeling guilty if there are any differences between you and your parents, and be wise about letting your children see any anger you might harbour regarding your upbringing. We shouldn't hide our anger, however, make sure you don't put your children in an awkward position. Something else to avoid is presenting our parents as perfect! That's not helpful either.

What it will give

Connection to our wider story helps to create deeper roots, even if there is pain in that story. Our children can learn so much about who they are by listening to their family's stories. Deeper roots give us a stronger base from which to grow our character, and they help us make more informed choices about how we develop. What other stories can you tell about the different generations, especially those that will highlight good character?

16. Annual appraisal

Over the last year, how have you improved regarding the ways you approach your sport?

Ways to ask it

I've gained so much from watching you play over the last year, and there have been so many highlights. I'm curious to know how you think you have improved over the last 12 months in the way you approach your sport? How have those steps forward improved your game?

What to try and avoid

This is a character question, not a coaching one. The number of goals or running speed is not our focus here. Instead, look at determination, sportsmanship, effort and responses to setbacks. However, this is not meant to be a guilt trip if your child has not progressed in these areas. Perhaps you could highlight times when progress was made.

What it will give

Growth involves more than winning and goals. This will give you the chance to help your child see how they are growing in the area that really matters – character. It reinforces that your child is not the 'finished' article. This also gives you the chance to think about the future, with follow-up questions such as, "Where would you like to develop next?", "What would help support your growth in these areas?" or "What would hinder that development?"

17. What's the big dream?

What are your sporting dreams and what will you need to get there?

Ways to ask it

I am thrilled to watch you play, but I've been wondering what your sporting dreams are. What sporting achievements will really give you a thrill? My dream is that you will always enjoy playing and taking part, but what is your dream? (You might want to write this one down with them.)

What to try and avoid

There are loads of dangers in this question. Number one: squashing their dream by saying or implying, "You'll never get that far." Number two: puffing up their ego with no reality by saying or implying, "You are the best, national captain should be your target." Number three: pushing your sporting dream for your children onto them, saying something like, "This is what I think you should aim for ..." Be willing to accept their answer and help them break it down, even if you are not sure about their response.

What it will give

The opportunity to get a feel for what your child really wants, and you'll be surprised at the range of answers they'll give. You'll also be able to help your child see how their character will help them achieve these goals. I encourage you to avoid making loads of comments focused on what they need to do. Instead, encourage them to sit down with you and their coach to talk about what is required in order to move forward.

18. Sticks and stones may break my bones, but bullying in sport is real

What does bullying look like in sport?

Ways to ask it

I know you have been told loads about bullying at school, but has anyone ever talked to you about what it looks like on the sports field? How could a fellow team member bully you? How could a coach or manager bully you?

What to try and avoid

This question may open a can of worms – good! Try to give examples of the actions of a coach or team member and ask your child to decide if it would constitute bullying. Most people don't realise that coaches shouting at players is a form of bullying and isn't acceptable. If your child describes being bullied themselves, try not to fly into action or anger (easier said than done). Listen and take notes and then consult the team's safeguarding policy.

What it will give

This will give your child an understanding of what boundaries are acceptable in sport. Having good character means having respect for yourself and the courage to speak out. This is never easy to do when you are being bullied. Having this conversation will make it clear to your child that you are open to talking about it with them. Should they go on to play professional sport, it's also essential they understand that bullying can happen to adults too.

Giving a positive understanding of self

19. Just a perfect day
Who is going to be perfect today?

Ways to ask it

As you prep for your game today, I'm wondering who is going to be perfect? Do you feel under pressure to be perfect and, if so, from whom? Why is it good for your game to know that it's not going to be perfect today? Is striving for perfection helpful or not? What can you do to be the best you can be? Do you want to know a time when I was not perfect recently, at home or work?

What to try and avoid

Fuelling the need for perfection in themselves, teammates, coaches, etc. Perfectionism is a high and crippling standard and it does not help us to grow a healthy character. Help your child to see that others on their team are not as perfect as they may think they are, and avoid presenting yourself as perfect, too. If it helps your child to open up, then be honest about a time when you were definitely not perfect.

What it will give

Honesty, humility and compassion are great character traits to discuss and pursue at the start of the day. They are significant in the creation of a strong character. If asked well, this question should take the pressure off and help your child aim for being their best. It should also encourage them to expect the best, but not perfection, from others, such as the referee, coach or team members. Placing ourselves under the pressure of perfection is a fast way to strip away the creativity and fun from a sport.

20. One of a kind
What makes your character unique?

Ways to ask it
There is no one like you. What makes your character unique? When you think about your team, what is unique about you? What unique strengths do you bring? Do you like change or consistent patterns? Do you like it loud or quiet? Do you think then speak or speak then think? Do you prefer time on your own or with others? What do those unique parts of who you are add to your team?

What to try and avoid
No character trait has more value than another. There is the danger that your children will look on in envy, wishing they were more like someone else. Comparison like this is unhelpful. Be prepared to list their character traits and why they are helpful. You might want to ask how they can draw deeper on them in order to be their best and benefit others.

What it will give
This question leads to an excellent understanding of self. With that knowledge comes the learning of our place in the world and what needs working on if we want to change that. If we can feel great about the unique person we are it will give us the courage to be the best version of us we can be and, when necessary, do the hard work of 'adding' to who we are.

21. All shapes and sizes
What are the advantages of your physique as you play today?

Ways to ask it
How might you use the benefits of your physique to your team's advantage? What do you need to work on to make the most of it? Everyone's physique is changing, what could that mean for the way you play over the coming years?

What to try and avoid
You are entering sensitive territory by starting a conversation involving children and body image, so be careful – but don't be scared! Avoid making unfavourable comparisons to others in the team. You are looking for positive physical attributes, so try bringing up specific moments in a game that highlight your child's. The other danger is that an early developer will always assume a physical advantage over others. They may not see the necessity of working on their game and challenging themselves to rely less on a physical edge that will disappear in the coming years. A discussion with any good coach will help the child feel excited about this challenge. The last pointer is not to compare our physique with those of professional adults who train for hours a week. It is important to remind children that they are not going to look like that (very few adults actually do!). If your child struggles to think of positives, don't rush to list them. Listen, ask questions and see if you can draw them out.

What it will give
Feeling good in our own skin is a gift. As we grow up and watch our bodies change, it's tough to feel completely good about who we are. That's why adopting a positive understanding about who we are is mega important. It will also give you a great insight into how your child feels about themselves.

22. What would your Top Trumps card say?

What do you bring to the side today?

Ways to ask it

I really enjoy watching you play and seeing you contribute to the team. If you were a Top Trumps card, what would the categories be and how would you score yourself? Perhaps you would have some from this list: stamina, work rate, decision-making, creativity, scoring, encouragement, sportsmanship.

What to try and avoid

Talking about their physical attributes, such as being strong or fast. These can be matched and bettered by others. It will be far better for your child's development to hear the character traits needed to access their strength, speed, etc.

What it will give

A massive opportunity to help your child see the value they bring. For example, "Your sportsmanship and your determination to use your strength. The hours of being faithful to practise, in order to be as fast as you are. The times you dusted yourself off to try and learn new ways to become faster." Feeling confident that they bring a valuable character trait to the team helps everyone perform with a smile on their face.

23. Pre-game chant!

What three positive things about yourself could you repeat quietly just before kick off?

Ways to ask it

Learning to tell yourself positive truths can help you relax and have fun. What three things could you say about yourself? If you were going to make up a chant about your strengths before the game, what would it sound like?

What to try and avoid

There is so much positive thinking rubbish out there, which only leads to myth and make believe. This is about making a grounded and honest list, not creating a fairy tale. If you come up with something unrealistic, when the bubble is popped – and it will be popped – the positive self-talk will become a tool of self-condemnation, which is seriously uncool! If you can make your chants about character traits it will be even more effective. For example, "I am committed, I am here for my teammates, I will be the best I can be."

What it will give

Obviously, the self-belief that comes with positive talk. However, it will also give you something useful to reflect and learn from after the game. On what occasions was your child committed? When did they support their teammates? When were they the best they could be? How might they get better at those things next week? Please note: you can reflect on these things regardless of the outcome of the game.

24. Warning: Mega-awkward conversation with your parent!

In what ways has entering your teenage years helped with your sport? In what ways hasn't it?

Ways to ask it

You don't have to answer this question if it's too personal, but in what ways has entering puberty helped with your sport and in what ways hasn't it? Becoming a teen means all sorts of changes. How have these changes affected your sport?

What to try and avoid

Body changes in puberty often create shame, so please don't add to this. Don't point out the changes your child has gone through – they know them well enough. Only you know how open you are as a family about talking about such things, so be honest about this topic in your own way. My plea is to go gentle, but please don't avoid it. Sorry if this question makes you feel uncomfortable, but it is an important one. Finally, don't be worried if your child doesn't give an answer.

What it will give

Being a teen and playing sport leads to a number of challenges, which are best talked about in a safe and open way. By asking the question, you are saying, "I'm willing to talk about anything." If they give you an answer, it will give you the opportunity to show acceptance and provide reassurance that what they are going through is normal and understandable. For us parents, nurturing the right character in our children means being willing to ask uncomfortable questions ourselves.

Nurturing a great team member

25. Pump up the team

How can you make the other team members feel valued?

Ways to ask it

If you were doing the coach's team talk today, what would you say to
help the team see what they bring to game day? What would you say
to each player? What music would play when you did this?

What to try and avoid

It doesn't matter if your child doesn't yet have the confidence to do
this face-to-face … helping them think through the team's assets
builds gratitude, and this is a beautiful and powerful character trait.
Again, avoid listing the physical attributes of team members.
Encourage your child to think deeper.

What it will give

People know when you value them. Someone who has spent time
thinking about the qualities of each team member will treat them
better, even if they don't do the team talk. This also provides a
chance for you to bang the drum regarding your child's strengths.

26. Jolly good sport

What will being a good sport look like today if you win? What will it look like if you lose?

Ways to ask it

After the game, if others call you a good sport, what will they have seen in order to give you that title? How does winning or losing affect the actions of a good sport? Does being a good sport mean you care less about being competitive?

What to try and avoid

There is a danger that your child might think you are suggesting they are not usually a good sport. Placing winning above being a good sport is also a danger for us parents. What value do you place on being a good one?

What it will give

Great character is not often diminished by either winning or losing, but this takes time to learn. Enabling both you and your child to reflect on being a good sport will prepare them for those moments when doing 'right' is tested on the sports pitch or by a boss. It will also give you the opportunity to squash the myth that being a good sport means caring less about the outcome of the game.

27. What's most precious around here?

In three words, what would you say are your team's biggest values?

Ways to ask it

You've gained so much from being part of your team, what do you think are their biggest values? Give me three words that sum up your team. Why are these important? How could you get better at living them out? Would you change them?

What to try and avoid

This is not a good time to have a bitching fest about team culture. If your child does struggle to see the positives, perhaps it's time to change clubs. If the team has strong values that are regularly promoted, challenge your child to describe them using different words. Ask them to give examples of where they are apparent.

What it will give

Helping your child to think about team culture is something the team is likely to have already done, but nevertheless, your conversations will help with their self-awareness and their awareness of their environment. This can lead to a better understanding of how these impact them. As a bonus, it will help increase their learning regarding what a good environment looks like and, conversely, how to identify a more challenging one.

28. Wounded soldier

What would you say to a teammate who is considering playing while injured?

Ways to ask it

If a teammate told you they had an injury, which they'd not informed the medical/coaching team about, how would you respond? What are they risking? Why do you think players are tempted to do that? Have you ever been tempted to do that?

What to try and avoid

I overheard a conversation between two players in a national team discussing just this. It happens, so go gently when listening to your child. They might be talking about a friend or themselves. This doesn't mean you have to agree, just be careful about the words you use in response.

What it will give

What are your views on playing when injured without seeking medical advice first? What if it was a final or an important selection game? These scenarios can be emotionally confusing. For me (and sports governing bodies), the risk is never worth it. As parents, we should be wise and strong in character by helping our children see the need to challenge a friend willing to play while injured (and challenge ourselves about playing injured), especially concerning unseen injuries such as concussion.

29. The referee's a ...

Tell me about today's referee? Why are they refereeing and what are they hoping for?

Ways to ask it

I love that people learn to be refs so you can play the game you love. Why are they refereeing and what are they hoping for? Are you going to make 100% right decisions today? Is the referee? What would being a good sport look like today with the referee? Let's role play a conversation with the ref that is respectful but still questioning. Can you blame the ref for losing?

What to try and avoid

Obviously, bad-mouthing previous referees. What are your views on them? What has your child learnt from you about them? Don't be surprised if a young person struggles to see the grey area and fails to recognise that referees can make mistakes too. It is worth remembering that blaming the result on a poor ref is a great way to mask asking honest questions about our own performance.

What it will give

Stressing about match officials is a waste of energy. Having the character to be grateful for those officials, even if they are having a bad day at the office, means that we are about to do our job better. Remember what it was like to have a nightmare boss? Did going on about it help? I've yet to meet a match official who doesn't love the game and enjoy seeing young people play the sport they love. Being abused and undermined by players, parents and coaches is not a great payoff for such passion. This conversation will hopefully improve sporting character.

Building self-awareness

30. Close Encounters of the Third Kind

If an alien arrived today, why should they play your sport?

Ways to ask it

OK, so this is a silly question, but the answer will help me to support you better. If an alien arrived today, why should they play your sport? If you met someone who'd never played a competitive game and they had all the choices you've had, what would you say to help convince them to play your chosen sport?

What to try and avoid

If you ask a silly question, you are likely to get some silly answers, so go with the flow. Try to hear what your child is saying about their sport and what motivates their engagement with it. Don't be afraid to probe if something is missing that you consider important, but avoid giving the impression that their answer is wrong just because it's not what you would have said.

What it will give

Hopefully, some fun, but it will also provide further insight into your child's 'why' when it comes to sport. You might be surprised about parts your child finds fun. Listening to their story should help you support their character growth by revealing why they play and helping them to see how this links to their character. That also means being ready to hear, "I like sport because you like it," or, "I play because you want me to play." Even harder, you may hear, "I don't like it and I don't want to play it anymore." All of these answers require a gentle response.

31. DJ Mum and Dad in da house!

Can I choose a motivational song to listen to?

Ways to ask it

Can I choose the song(s) to listen to on the way to the game? Why do you think I picked them? What helps you prep for a match? What songs have the messages you want to hear on the way to a game? Did you know that I have to get myself pumped before doing something important at work? What do you think I do to motivate myself?

What to try and avoid

This is not meant to be too intense, nor is it meant to become a massive debate about music genres! (Prepare before you ask this question by picking a song with positive elements that can be used as good self-talk.)

What it will give

Fun, hopefully. The journey to the match should be relaxed, normal and enjoyable. A good DJ battle will help with this. It will also give an insight into what your child finds helpful, and what can help you fuel the positive self-talk that is needed before a competition.

32. What am I going to brag about?
What do you think will make me proud of you today?

Ways to ask it
You know how I love watching you play. Well, what is it that will
make me proud of you today? Watching you compete gives me so
much pleasure. What parts of watching you do you think will provide
me with the most joy?

What to try and avoid
We know that others are obsessed with them, however, talk of results
and outcomes when linked with measurements of pride are not
constructive. Sorry to say this, but they are not important at this age, and
they are doubly unimportant to the parent-child relationship. In fact, they
are somewhat toxic and can help create an unhealthy (fixed) mindset.

What it will give
So many parents brag on social media about score lines and trophies.
It's time to help your children see what really makes you proud. Talk
about fun and the type of person they are, such as: their attitude to
change, their humility in success and the way they are as a team
player. This is where you'll fuel the belief that no matter what
happens on the sports field, they are more than a loss or a win to you
– it's their character that's the most important. Ask this question
before the game so they'll go into it relaxed in the knowledge that you
will be proud of them regardless of outcome.

33. When it all gets a bit tense!
Which are you: fight, flight or freeze?

Ways to ask it
We all handle stress and conflict in different ways, which do you
think you are: fight, flight or freeze? Which do you think I am? In
what ways does that reaction help or hinder you? What can you do to
make a more reasoned judgment in those situations? (Breathing, self-
distraction, talking to someone?)

What to try and avoid
Blaming children for their natural responses ... we act automatically
before we have even considered it.

What it will give
This will help children to understand that their responses to stress
and pressure are normal. Building character is about working with our
natural responses and learning to manage them. This conversation
will build self-awareness and the ability to nurture character. It will
also provide you with the opportunity to talk about the good and bad
ways you handle your stress.

34. Who is in control?

What can and can't you control today?

Ways to ask it

As you get yourself ready, what do you think you are in control of?
What is beyond your control?

What to try and avoid

This is deep learning. Children (and vast numbers of adults) love to
think they are in control of way more than they are. If they give the
textbook answer 'just myself', give them some scenarios and ask them
how they might 'control' their own character and mindset in those
situations. For example, a substantial loss, a dodgy ref, being subbed
off or being isolated by their teammates in the game.

What it will give

The chance to correctly size things up on competition day. So much
energy and emotion can be wasted on trying to control and
manipulate that which is beyond our influence. Then, when we are
presented with an opportunity that is under our control, we're often
too stressed or mentally knackered to take it. Learning to meditate
and reflect on what we can and can't control brings great freedom.

35. Learning outcomes

What would winning or losing teach you today?

Ways to ask it

Today is an excellent opportunity for you to grow as a person. What would winning or losing teach you? They both have value and offer the opportunity to learn. What might prevent you learning these lessons?

What to try and avoid

Blame, self-doubt and arrogance are all risks here. There is a danger of your child coming to the conclusion that a player is amazing and deserves to win, or is a victim and should give up. Focusing on character will help avoid these pitfalls.

What it will give

Learning to treat each success and stumble as an opportunity to learn makes up the mindset required to excel in life. If we can set the expectation of learning rather than winning, we will help our children develop the type of creative thinking needed to face the challenges life throws our way. Ask yourself whether you're open to learning or do you feel that it's the winning that matters most?

36. It's been emotional

Sport can make us feel really great and also really low sometimes. What would help you when these low feelings come?

Ways to ask it
What have been your biggest emotional highs and lows in sport over the last year? What helped you stay grounded in the highs and keep going during the lows? What would you like me to do when those low times come? Can you avoid emotional pain in sport? What are the moments that cause you the most pain?

What to try and avoid
The challenge with emotions is that we try to fix them or rush to give our children the answers on how to handle them. Before asking this question, ask yourself how you view low emotional times? It is natural to want to prevent our children from experiencing pain, but it is helpful for them. If they are not sure what to do with negative feelings, help them problem solve rather than spoon-feeding them the answers. Follow up with questions such as, "It's OK not to know how you would handle this. Where could you find out more?" or "When have you seen others cope well with feeling low?"

What it will give
Great character is not about putting on a strong front for show when you're feeling low, it's about knowing how to manage yourself and seek support from others. This conversation will give you the opportunity to look at a topic that is rarely discussed in the open. It's something that is essential to maintaining great character, both on and off the sports field.

Questions to pose on the way home

37. The post-match interview
How was it for you?

Ways to ask it
I got so much from today, but I was wondering how it was for you?
I loved your work rate and effort. What do you think about how you
played? For a bit of fun, do a Sky/BT Sport style interview. Get them
to focus on fellow team members and the opposition.

What to try and avoid
This is all about letting your child express their view about what
happened. They could win and be miserable, they could lose and be
ecstatic. Avoid asking them questions such as, "Did you have fun?"
and "You played really well, didn't you?" These questions really only
have one answer and to keep you happy your children are likely to
feel they should say they agree with you even if deep down they don't.
If you do disagree with their answer, ask another question to help
them articulate things themselves. For example, if they say, "I played
rubbish," ask them to give you an example of this and question
whether they think they played badly for the whole match. Then
challenge them by pointing out a time when, in your opinion, they
played well.

What it will give
Personally, I've had so many surprise answers to this question that I
wouldn't think of using another one. It gives you the chance to hear
about what's important to your child and to get a feel for their
emotional state, perspective and logic. You'll also get an excellent
insight into your child's character, which will help you decide what to
do next. Sometimes, it's right to ask questions that lead to growth and
reflection, other times you will see that they are too tired to talk
anymore, so just thank them for their previous answers and leave it there.

38. They are not the enemy!

What character traits did you see in the other team members/players that you liked?

Ways to ask it

I enjoyed watching you play and seeing the passion from both sets of supporters. If you were the opposition's coach today, what encouraging comments would you have made after the game? Where did they show great character?

What to try and avoid

It's unhelpful to talk the opposition down or become fixated on what your child didn't like about them. Listen to your child and then either redirect the conversation or bring them back to the question.

What it will give

The strength of character to be willing to see the good in the opposition and to learn from them is a lifelong gift. Both teammates and opponents can spur us on to get better at what we do. This reduces how much we feel the need to compare ourselves to others or be intimidated by them. Instead, we find them inspirational.

39. Sport is the teacher and you are the student

What did you learn about yourself today?

Ways to ask it

I am curious about what you learnt about yourself today and how you respond to challenges. What did you learn that will help you grow as a person? What did you learn that will help you as an adult?

What to try and avoid

If they can't see what they learnt or need to learn that's fine, but don't come in with a long list of lessons you think they should have absorbed. Ask some more open questions and leave it there.

What it will give

Being willing to learn is about accepting that we can change and that we have control over many parts of our attitude and character. Having a non-fixed mindset is one of the most significant gifts we can give our children. Even if they can't find an answer to this question, asking your child to reflect on their potential for growth will set them up for the creative and flexible mindset required to be successful both on and off the sports pitch.

40. Silence is golden, golden

" " (Silence)

Ways to ask it

This is for those moments when your child is in pain. Merely thank them for being honest or place a comforting hand on their shoulder. Alternatively, stop the car, give them a hug and say nothing.

What to try and avoid

Speaking honestly, us parents like to try and put out the fire of emotional pain quicker than an 18-year-old will put a photo of their dinner on social media. The key here is to listen and provide comfort. Yes, there will be a time for questions and a time to ask about learning and the next steps, but for now let the emotions be expressed and heard and avoid rushing into providing solutions.

What it will give

Emotion is better expressed than repressed and quickly swept under the carpet. People of character are not afraid of their emotions and are wise enough to give them the time to be expressed. As parents, there will be many moments of pain in your child's sporting life, both on and off the pitch. Giving them permission to be honest, with the knowledge that their home is a place where they can pour their heart out, is essential.

Bonus question

41. One last question

How well are you doing at modelling the character you are hoping to nurture in your child?

I'm not expecting you to be perfect – as I said earlier, I am not called the Non-Perfect Dad without good reason. However, I need to be honest and tell you that your children will learn far more from parents with a hunger to grow their own character than they will from 40 well-written questions and a parent living the opposite. The 'winning' combination is a parent willing to expand on who they are and pose questions like these. Then you have fertile ground for courageously honest parents to nurture the character that will support success both on and off the sports field.